P9-CEL-051

Turbulent Planet

Violent Skies

Hurricanes

Chris Oxlade

Chicago, Illinois

For information, address the publisher:
Raintree, 100 N. LaSalle, Suite 1200, Chicago, IL 60602
Customer Service: 888-363-4266
Visit our website at www.raintreelibrary.com

Printed and bound in China by South China Printing Company.
08 07 06 05 04
10 9 8 7 6 5 4 3 2 1

Library of Congress Cataloging-in-Publication Data
Oxlade, Chris.
  Violent skies : hurricanes / Chris Oxlade.
    p. cm. -- (Turbulent planet)
  Includes bibliographical references and index.
  ISBN 1-4109-1100-4 (lib. bdg.) -- ISBN 1-4109-1205-1 (pbk.) 1.
Hurricanes--Juvenile literature. I. Title. II. Series.
  QC944.2.O95 2004
  551.55'2--dc22

2004014646

Photo acknowledgments
The publishers would like to thank the following for permission to reproduce photographs: p. 4/5, Frank Lane Picture Agency; p. 5 top, Science Photo Library/NASA/Goddard Space Flight Center; p. 5 middle, Corbis/Annie Griffiths Belt; p. 5 bottom, Corbis/Jim McDonald; p. 7, Science Photo Library/Carl Purcell; p. 7 right, Science Photo Library/James Stevenson; p. 8, Science Photo Library/Fritz Henle; p. 9, Science Photo Library/ NOAA; p. 10/11, Corbis/Stocktrek; p. 11, Corbis/Roger Ball; p. 12, Panos Pictures/Trygve Bolstad; p. 13, Panos Pictures/ Fred Hoogervorst; p. 14/15, Frank Lane Picture Agency/ Colin Marshall; p. 14, Frank Lane Picture Agency; p. 16, Corbis/ Lester Lefkowitz; p. 17, Corbis/NASA; p. 18, Corbis; p. 18, left, Science Photo Library/Chris Saltlberger; p. 19, Corbis; p. 20, Science Photo Library/2002 Orbital Imaging Corporation; p. 21, Science Photo Library/NASA; p. 21 right, Corbis/NASA; p. 22, Corbis Sygma; p. 23, Science Photo Library/Chris Saltlberger; p. 24/25, Guy Motil/Corbis; p. 24, Corbis/Bettmann; p. 25, Corbis/Steve Starr; p. 26/27, Corbis/ Galen Rowell; p. 27, Frank Lane Picture Agency; p. 28, Corbis/Jim McDonald; p. 29, Corbis/Post and Courier; p. 29 right, Corbis/Alan Schein; p. 30/31, Corbis Sygma; p. 30, Corbis/Annie Griffiths Belt; p. 31, Corbis; p. 32, Corbis Sygma; p. 33, Corbis/Will & Deni McIntyre; p. 34, Corbis/ Steve Starr; p. 34 left, Corbis; p. 35 Corbis Sygma; p. 36/37, Corbis Sygma/Tramontina Gary; p. 37, Corbis/Roger Ressmeyer; p. 38, Science Photo Library/NASA/Goddard Space Flight Center; p. 38 left, Corbis/John Van Hasselt; p. 39, Corbis/Yan Arthus-Bertrand; p. 40/41, Corbis Sygma; p. 40, Corbis; p. 41, Science Photo Library/Detlev Ravensway; p. 42, Corbis/Kristin Royalty; p. 43, Corbis; p. 44, Corbis Sygma; p. 45, Corbis/Stocktrek.

Cover photograph reproduced with permission of Associated Press.

Every effort has been made to contact copyright holders of any material reproduced in this book. Any omissions will be rectified in subsequent printings if notice is given to the publishers.

Disclaimer
All the Internet addresses (URLs) given in this book were valid at the time of going to press. However, due to the dynamic nature of the Internet, some addresses may have changed, or sites may have changed or ceased to exist since publication. While the author and publishers regret any inconvenience this may cause readers, no responsibility for any such changes can be accepted by either the author or the publishers.

The paper used to print this book comes from sustainable resources.

Contents

Any words appearing in the text in bold, **like this,** are explained in the glossary. You can also look out for them in the "Wet Words" box at the bottom of each page.

A Swirling Storm

It is late summer in the Caribbean. Usually the sea is calm here, but not today. Monster waves are crashing onto the **shore**. There must be powerful winds out at sea. Soon the sky fills with threatening clouds. The wind starts to blow and heavy rain begins to fall. A hurricane is on the way!

Winds and waves

The winds grow stronger and stronger. It is hard to walk outside. Sheets of **torrential** rain come down. The winds tear things apart. **Debris** from damaged houses, fences, and road signs flies around. The sea level rises quickly. Huge waves **surge** over the **coast**. They smash down houses, wash away cars and buses, and carry boats **inland**. It is **chaos** everywhere. The terrifying weather lasts for many hours.

The hurricane slowly moves away. A few hours later, the sky is blue and the sea is calm again. Behind it is a trail of flooding and destruction.

> " The city looks like a giant garbage dump. "
>
> A man from Darwin, Australia, after **Cyclone** Tracy 1974

Hurricane Bonnie arrives at Wilmington Beach, North Carolina in 1998. ▷

cyclone   name given to a hurricane in the southern hemisphere
debris   bits and pieces of wrecked houses, cars, and other objects

What does a hurricane look like?

*What is a **storm surge**?*

What can you do if a hurricane is coming?

Destructive hurricanes

The strongest winds on Earth belong to **tornadoes,** but hurricanes cause more damage and affect more people. A hurricane can grow to hundreds of miles across. Near the center, its winds blow at more than 150 miles (240 kilometers) per hour. The winds destroy things in the hurricane's path and push up huge waves. These cause terrible floods.

surge   sudden rush
tornado   spinning column of air that makes contact with the ground

Ocean Storms

A hurricane is a huge, swirling storm. Inside are very strong winds and rains. **Meteorologists** call these storms **tropical** storms. A tropical storm becomes a hurricane when the winds inside it blow faster than 73 miles (118 kilometers) per hour.

Hurricane hot spots

Luckily, you will probably never be in a hurricane. This is because hurricanes only happen in a few parts of the world. They form over very warm seas and oceans in the tropics. That is why they are called tropical storms. Hurricanes move away from the **equator** until they hit colder water or land. Then they die away.

This map shows the areas that are most often hit by hurricanes as well as the places mentioned in this book.

equator   imaginary line around Earth, halfway between the poles
eye   area in the center of a hurricane where the winds are calm

More names

Strong tropical storms develop in the Atlantic and the Caribbean Sea. Here they are called hurricanes. In the western North Pacific and China Sea, they are called **typhoons**. Strong tropical storms appear in the Indian Ocean and Australia, too. These are called tropical **cyclones**. In this book, we normally use the word *hurricane*. Everything we say about hurricanes is true for typhoons and tropical cyclones, too.

Fifteen million trees were blown down during Great Britain's Great Storm in 1987. ▽

The Great Storm

The Great Storm hit southern Britain in 1987. Although there were winds as strong as those in a hurricane, it was not a hurricane. A hurricane has an **eye,** but this weather system did not.

Waves and high winds from Hurricane Gilbert batter ◁ Jamaica in 1988.

meteorologist   scientist who studies and reports on the weather
tropical   in the area of the world, near the equator, where the weather is warm

Hurricane seasons

Hurricanes only form at certain times of the year. These times are called hurricane **seasons.** In the northern **hemisphere,** the hurricane season lasts from June to November. These are the summer and fall months. By June, the sea has warmed up enough for hurricanes to form. After November, the sea has cooled down again. A hurricane is most likely to strike in August and September. In the southern hemisphere, it is summer and fall between November and May. This is the hurricane season there.

Never used again

If a hurricane is very damaging, like Hurricane Hugo, its name is never used again. The name is retired and replaced by a new one.

The name *Hugo* was given to the hurricane that caused this damage. It went on to be the strongest hurricane of 1989. ▷

hemisphere   one half of Earth
season   time of the year with typical weather

Hurricane names

Meteorologists give each new hurricane, **typhoon,** or **tropical cyclone** a name. The names identify the different hurricanes. Simple names are easier for people to remember in hurricane warnings. Meteorologists start a new list of names at the beginning of each year. This is in alphabetical order. The first hurricane of the year gets the first name on the list, the second one the second name, and so on. There are separate lists for each hurricane area. The list for hurricanes in the Atlantic is made up of boys and girls names. The list for the North Pacific is made up of names of animals and plants. About ten names are used up in the Atlantic region each year.

Pick a name

This is the 2005 hurricane name list for the Atlantic:

Arlene, Bret, Cindy, Dennis, Emily, Franklin, Gert, Harvey, Irene, Jose, Katrina, Lenny, Maria, Nate, Ophelia, Philippe, Rita, Stan, Tammy, Vince, Wilma.

This is a rare sighting of two hurricanes in the Pacific in 1974. Hurricane Ione is at the top and Hurricane Kirsten is at the bottom.

Hurricane Andrew

A **tropical** storm began over the Atlantic Ocean on August 17, 1992. Hurricane **forecasters** named it Andrew. Hurricane Andrew moved slowly westward. By August 22 the storm was about 500 miles (800 kilometers) from the **coast** of the United States. It was a **severe** storm, but not a hurricane. People were not too worried. The next day, Andrew became more powerful and changed direction. It battered the Bahamas. Then, it got even stronger. With winds blowing at more than 150 miles (240 kilometers) per hour, it headed straight for Florida.

◁ This is a map showing the path of Hurricane Andrew.

Hurricane Andrew damage

- 61 lives lost
- 20,000 homes destroyed
- 60,000 homes badly damaged
- 200,000 people made homeless
- $25 billion of damage

These **satellite** images of Hurricane Andrew show how it developed as it moved westward across the Atlantic. ▷

broadcast   send information over the radio or television
forecaster   person who gives information about the weather

Andrew hits land

Hurricane warnings were **broadcast** for the southern tip of Florida. More than one million people abandoned their homes and drove north to safety. Hurricane Andrew reached land in the early morning of August 24. The **eye** of the storm hit the southern **suburbs** of the city of Miami.

The sea level rose by 16.4 feet (5 meters). Huge waves flooded **inland.** They wrecked homes and stores. The waves picked up boats and dumped them in the streets. Gusts of wind were measured at more than 200 miles (320 kilometers) per hour. The wind ripped thousands of mobile homes to pieces. Vehicles were flipped over like toys. Millions of trees were flattened.

The hurricane went into the Gulf of Mexico. It damaged oil rigs at sea. Then it hit the coast of Louisiana, causing more damage.

> " Then I drove toward Homestead. I was only halfway there when I began seeing the totally **unbelievable destruction.** "
>
> An insurance inspector visiting Homestead, a town south of Miami

△ These are the remains of mobile homes in a park. They were in the path of Hurricane Andrew.

severe   very bad or serious
suburb   area of houses on the edge of a city

11

Bangladesh cyclones

Whenever **cyclones** hit the country of Bangladesh, it suffers badly. Most of Bangladesh is made up of a huge **delta**. This is a low-lying area where many rivers flow into the sea. Millions of poor farmers live and work on Bangladesh's deltas.

Cyclones often move through the Bay of Bengal and land in Bangladesh. Waves **surge** across the delta and cause terrible flooding. Poor **communications** make it difficult to warn people. Bad roads delay their escape.

Dangerous floods

People often talk about the strong winds of hurricanes. But flooding along the coast causes the most deaths. The cyclones in Bangladesh show this.

Flooding in the streets of Dhaka, △ the capital of Bangladesh, in 1998.

communication   way of giving and receiving information
delta   wide, fan-shaped piece of land, where a river empties into the sea

Cyclone 2B

The giant storm known as Cyclone 2B hit Bangladesh on April 29, 1991. Its winds blew at a speed of 145 miles (235 kilometers) per hour. A wall of seawater 20 feet (6 meters) high surged across the low lying **coast.** Warnings were given on national radio. Thousands of people squeezed into hurricane shelters, but millions were left outside. The winds and waves destroyed more than a million homes. Tens of thousands of people were drowned. They could not escape to higher ground. Altogether, 140,000 people died. Since this disaster, more hurricane shelters have been built in Bangladesh.

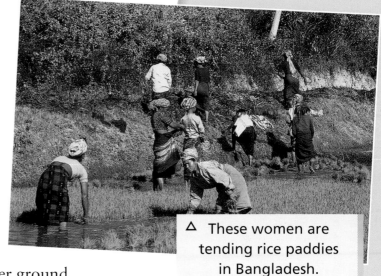

△ These women are tending rice paddies in Bangladesh.

The damage caused by cyclones in Bangladesh is so great because it is a very poor country. It also has a large **population.** Warning systems are not as advanced as they are as in wealthier parts of the world.

Hurricane facts

A cyclone hit Bangladesh in 1970. Giant waves swept across the delta. They destroyed millions of rice **paddies.** Millions of cattle were drowned, too. About 300,000 people died. This was one of the worst natural disasters ever to happen in the world.

NEPAL
BHUTAN
Brahmaputra River
Ganges River
BANGLADESH
INDIA
Dhaka ○
○ Chittagong
○ Cox's Bazaar
BAY OF BENGAL
MYANMAR
N
Path of Cyclone 2B
200 miles
200 kilometers

◁ This is a map of Bangladesh. Cyclones sweep in from the Bay of Bengal.

paddy   water-filled field used for growing rice
population   total number of people living in a place

Hurricane Science

Hurricanes bring damaging, violent winds and heavy rain, but they start their lives in warm places. They begin over **tropical** seas and oceans. Sunshine is always very strong in the tropics. The strong sunshine heats the surfaces of seas and oceans. The water gets very warm. This means it contains heat **energy**. Hurricanes need this energy to form and keep going.

Hurricane from above

A hurricane is a huge storm. From above, a hurricane looks like a big, white swirl with the dark ocean underneath. Around the edges are ragged, spiraling arms of cloud. Right in the middle is an area called the **eye**. Inside the eye, the winds are calm.

Small and deadly

Bad does not always mean big! **Cyclone** Tracy was very **compact**. At 30 mi (48 km) from the eye, the winds were light, but the center of the storm destroyed Darwin, Australia.

◁ This shows the devastation in Darwin created when Cyclone Tracy swept through the town in 1974.

compact   packed closely together
cumulonimbus   enormous thunder clouds up to 32,800 ft (10 km) high

Hurricane structure

Huge, towering thunderclouds make up a hurricane. These can be thousands of feet high. They are called **cumulonimbus** clouds. The storm clouds form into round bands, with spaces between them. There may be hundreds of **severe** thunderstorms inside a hurricane. Lightning flashes through the clouds and **torrential** rain pours out of them.

This is what the inside of a hurricane looks like. The arrow shows the direction ▽ it is spinning.

surface of the sea

Hurricane sizes

A typical hurricane is about 300 mi (480 km) across. Some are as big as 600 mi (960 km) across. They are more than 5 mi (8 km) high.

△ This is Fiji in the Pacific Ocean. The tropical storms that turn into hurricanes form over warm seas like this.

energy source that provides power
torrential like a torrent, which is a rushing stream of liquid

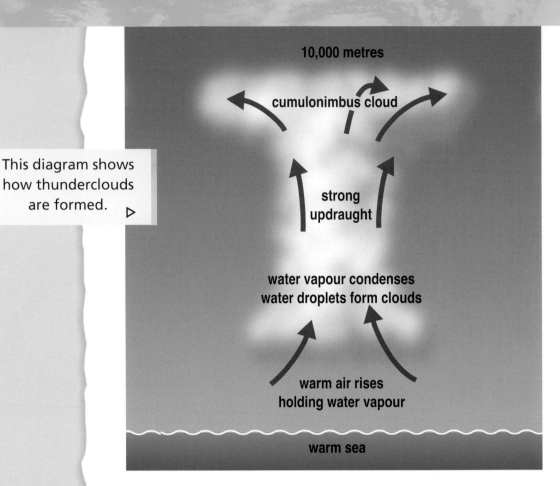

10,000 metres

cumulonimbus cloud

strong
updraught

water vapour condenses
water droplets form clouds

warm air rises
holding water vapour

warm sea

This diagram shows
how thunderclouds
are formed. ▷

Hurricane formation

The water temperature must be at least 80 °F (27 °C) before a
hurricane can form. The warm seawater heats the air above
its surface. The warm air is good at holding **water vapor.**
A lot of water **evaporates** from the water surface into the air.
The warm air is very moist.

Storm energy

Hurricanes have
lots of **energy.**
Scientists have
figured out how
much energy
a hurricane
makes in one
day. It is enough
electricity to
run the United
States for six
months.

The incredible
energy in a
hurricane would
run the millions of
lights of Las Vegas
◁ for many years.

condense   turn from gas into liquid
evaporate   turn from liquid to gas

Forming clouds

Warm air always rises upward, if there is cooler air around and above it. You can see this effect when hot, smoky air rises from a bonfire. The warm, moist air over the warm ocean rises and slowly cools. The water vapor **condenses** to form tiny water droplets. The same thing happens when you breathe on a cold mirror. The water droplets collect together and form clouds over the ocean.

Towering storms

When the water vapor condenses, it gives out heat. This heat keeps the air warm, and the air continues to rise. The rising air forms strong **updrafts.** The updrafts only stop when they reach about 32,800 feet (10,000 meters) above the surface. Incredibly high **cumulonimbus** clouds are formed.

Hurricane seedlings

A **seedling** is a group of thunderstorms. These may turn into a hurricane. About 100 seedlings form over the Atlantic each year. Only about one in ten of them becomes a **tropical** storm. About half of these tropical storms become hurricanes, **typhoons,** or **cyclones.**

A group of thunderstorms over an ocean, seen from a **satellite** high in space.

The eye of the storm

There is always a calm area right in the center of a hurricane. It is called the **eye.** The eye is very small compared to the hurricane. Normally it is between 5 and 15 miles (8 and 24 kilometers) across. Some eyes are as small as 3 miles (5 kilometers) across and some are as large as 40 miles (64 kilometers) across. The eye is a strange place. If you travel toward the middle of a hurricane, the winds get faster and faster, but in the eye the wind is calm. The air is also clear. From above you can see straight through the hurricane to the ocean below. On the water's surface are violent, giant waves. They are caused by the violent winds around the eye.

△ This is inside the eye of Hurricane Floyd. It was photographed in 1999 from the aircraft of a hurricane-hunting team.

△ The eye of Hurricane Isabel was photographed from the International Space Station in September 2003.

The eye wall

Inside the eye, it is like being inside a giant tin can. Circular walls of cloud up to 32,800 feet (10 kilometers) high surround you. This wall of cloud is called the **eye wall.** It is made up of towering thunderclouds. The hurricane's most violent winds are in the clouds of the eye wall. The smaller the eye, the stronger the winds are. The severe thunderstorms in the eye wall often cause **tornadoes** to form. Tornadoes have winds even stronger than hurricanes. Sometimes seabirds fly around in the eye. They are trapped there because they cannot fly through the violent winds in the eye wall.

Hurricane Camille

The smaller the eye, the more violent the winds around it. Hurricane Camille hit Mississippi in 1969. Up to that year, it was the most violent hurricane to hit the United States. Its eye was just 4 miles (7 kilometers) across.

This damage was caused by Hurricane Camille's winds. They reached more than 200 miles (320 kilometers) per hour.

Spinning storms

A **seedling** thunderstorm cannot turn into a hurricane right away. It must become a **tropical** storm first. A tropical storm is a huge spinning storm, but its winds are weaker than the winds of a hurricane. Only a few seedlings turn into a tropical storm. Most just die away. This happens because of the way Earth **rotates.**

If a seedling storm forms close to the **equator,** it quickly dies away. But at **latitudes** more than five degrees away from the equator, the storm seedling begins to spin slowly. It moves slowly westward. This is because Earth is rotating.

A storm near Australia in the southern hemisphere, spins clockwise. ▽

The Coriolis effect

Think about a wind blowing to the north, toward the North Pole. Instead of blowing in a straight line, it follows a curved path over Earth's surface. This is because of the spin of Earth and the **atmosphere.** This is called the Coriolis effect. It explains why storms begin to rotate.

This diagram shows the curved path of winds over Earth's surface. ▽

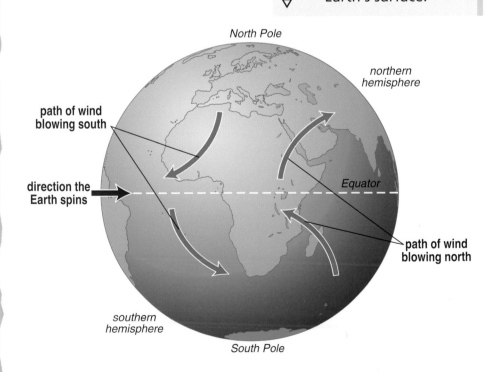

North Pole

northern hemisphere

path of wind blowing south

direction the Earth spins

Equator

path of wind blowing north

southern hemisphere

South Pole

clockwise   direction that the hands of a clock move around
counterclockwise   moving in the opposite direction to the hands of a clock

Storm to hurricane

Warm, moist air goes into the storm. Its **energy** makes the storm spin faster. The storm's winds increase. If the winds reach 39 miles (62 kilometers) per hour or more, the storm is known as a tropical storm. The storm keeps growing as long as there is warm, moist air to feed it. If it moves farther from the equator, it spins faster and faster. When its winds reach 73 miles (118 kilometers) per hour, then it is officially a hurricane. Only about half of all tropical storms become hurricanes. Tropical storms always rotate **counterclockwise** if they develop in the northern **hemisphere**. In the southern hemisphere, they always rotate **clockwise**.

This thunderstorm is dying away.

This photograph of Hurricane Fran over the Caribbean Sea in the northern hemisphere shows it is spinning counterclockwise. ▽

Dying storms

Most tropical storms and hurricanes die out before they hit land. Some move over cool seas and lose their supply of energy. Others move close to the equator, where there is nothing to keep them spinning.

latitude   distance north or south of the equator, measured in degrees
rotate   turn around or twist

Hurricane Measurements

Meteorologists measure the speed and direction of wind, rainfall, **air pressure,** and temperature. But how do they measure hurricanes? The answer is by their strength, or **intensity.** The intensity measures how strong the winds are and how much damage the hurricane does when it reaches land.

Rare hurricanes

Very **severe** hurricanes are rare. Only four category 5 hurricanes hit the United States in the 20th century.

The category 4 Hurricane Luis battered Guadeloupe in the Caribbean in 1995.

▽

air pressure   force of air pressing down on Earth
category   group or class of things

The Saffir-Simpson Scale

The **international** scale for measuring hurricanes is the Saffir-Simpson hurricane scale. There are five **categories** of hurricanes in this scale. Category 1 is the weakest, or least intense. Category 5 is the strongest, or most intense. The wind speeds in the list are **sustained** wind speeds. This means the winds blow at this speed most of the time during the worst part of the storm.

Staff members at the National Hurricane Center in the U.S. watch the progress of Hurricane Floyd. This hurricane reached category 4 strength▷

The Saffir-Simpson Scale

Category	Wind speed	Damage
1	73–94 miles (118–152 kilometers) per hour	Not much damage to buildings. Some trees fall. Mobile homes move. Some flooding on **coasts.**
2	95–109 miles (153–176 kilometers) per hour	Roofs, doors, and windows broken. Many trees fall. Piers damaged. Small boats swept ashore. Flooding of low-lying coasts.
3	110–129 miles (177–208 kilometers) per hour	Structures of buildings damaged. Mobile homes destroyed. Flooding up to 6.2 miles (10 kilometers) **inland.**
4	130–154 miles (209–248 kilometers) per hour	Some roofs torn off and walls collapse. **Erosion** of beaches. Large boats swept inland. Severe flooding up to 6.2 miles (10 kilometers) inland.
5	more than 154 miles (248 kilometers) per hour	Some buildings destroyed by wind. Buildings near coast swept away by waves. Severe flooding up to 10 miles (16 kilometers) inland.

erosion   wearing away by action of water or wind
sustain   keep at a certain strength or level all the time

Hurricane winds

Hurricanes are famous for their winds. A **category** 5 hurricane has **sustained** wind speeds of more than 154 mi (248 km) per hour around its **eye.** Gusts of winds can reach 200 mi (320 km) per hour. There are mini **tornadoes** in the **eye wall.** These have even stronger winds. When the strong winds blow across many miles of ocean, they create huge waves. In the Pacific, the waves can be 82 ft (25 m) high. This is the same height as a six-story building. These waves can cover even the biggest ships.

Fifi floods

Hurricane Fifi hit Central America in 1974. Torrential rain fell on Honduras, El Salvador, Guatemala, and Belize. About 25 in. (63 cm) of rain fell in a day. Floods and **landslides** killed 8,000 people.

◁ Houses in Honduras were surrounded by muddy flood waters after Hurricane Fifi passed by.

A hurricane's winds create dangerous waves. ▷

flash flood   quickly developing flood
inland   away from the coast

Twenty-foot (6-m) waves crash against the shore on Palm Beach, Florida. ▷

Surge heights

A hurricane storm surge can easily reach 16.4 ft (5 m) high. The highest recorded storm surge measured about 43 ft (13 m). It hit Australia in 1899.

The storm surge

The **air pressure** in the center of a hurricane is lower than the air pressure outside the hurricane. This is because the air is rising in the center. This low pressure allows the water underneath the hurricane to push upward. This makes a wide bulge in the sea's surface. The bulge is made higher by the wind. The wind pushes the bulge forward, ahead of the storm. When a hurricane hits a **coast,** the water washes right over low-lying land. This rush of water is called a **storm surge.** It is the most dangerous feature of a hurricane.

Rain storms

A big hurricane can pick up 2.2 billion tons of water a day through **evaporation** from the sea. This water falls back to Earth as **torrential** rain. A hurricane can drop a year's worth of rain in a few hours. If this happens over land, the rain causes **flash floods.**

Moving a city

In 1961 Hurricane Hattie caused a storm surge. This destroyed 75 percent of the buildings in Belize City, the capital of Belize in Central America. Two hundred people died. A new capital city, Belmopan, was built 50 mi (80 km) **inland.** There, it is safe from future hurricanes.

storm surge   sudden rise in sea level that happens as a hurricane approaches land

A Hurricane Is Coming

What is it like to be in the path of a **category** 4 hurricane? What would you do to protect yourself from this monster storm? What happens to towns and cities when a hurricane thunders through? How do places **recover** afterward? Let us see what happens when a hurricane forms and hits the southern **coast** of the United States.

Storms at sea

A group of thunderstorms forms over the warm, **tropical** ocean, near the west coast of Africa. It is a hurricane **seedling.** It is more than 1,000 miles (1,600 kilometers) from the United States. It will take over a week to arrive there. However, images from weather **satellites** show it exists. The seedling is being watched!

Hurricane facts

Typhoon Tip (1979) holds the record for the tropical storm with the most energy inside it. Luckily, it never reached land. It died out over the Pacific Ocean.

Map to show the path △ of our category 4 hurricane.

data   information, usually in the form of facts or statistics
recover   get better

Gaining strength

Gradually the seedling begins to spin. It turns from several groups of storms into one large spinning storm. A few days later, it has grown into a tropical storm. Hurricane **forecasters** watch it closely on their satellite images. It is moving westward at 15 miles (24 kilometers) per hour. Each day it spins faster, as it takes **energy** from the warm sea. Finally, a small area appears in the storm's center. It is an **eye.** A new hurricane has formed!

Hurricane forecasters send aircraft to measure conditions inside the hurricane. **Data** from the aircraft shows that winds near the eye are blowing at more than 100 miles (160 kilometers) per hour. Ships sail north or south to avoid the approaching storm.

This group of thunderstorm clouds could be the start of a new hurricane. ▽

Shipping disaster
During World War II, the U.S. Pacific Third Fleet sailed into the middle of a typhoon in the Pacific Ocean. The ships were tossed around like toys. Three ships sank and others were **severely** damaged. Eight hundred sailors died.

△ The deck of an American aircraft carrier damaged by a typhoon in the Pacific Ocean in 1945.

satellite   object that observes Earth from space

The hurricane continues on its path toward the United States. About 36 hours before a hurricane is likely to hit land, **forecasters broadcast** a hurricane watch on television and radio. Most people know exactly what to do. They begin their family disaster plans.

Disaster supply kit

People in hurricane hot spots keep a supply kit handy. It might contain:

- canned foods
- camping stove
- pans
- blankets
- wet-weather clothes
- first-aid kit
- flashlight and spare batteries
- radio and spare batteries
- money
- tools
- drinking water.

Disaster plan

- Put strong wooden shutters over the windows.
- Lock away loose objects such as lawn chairs.
- Check the contents of disaster supply kits.
- Store plenty of water in containers.
- Buy enough food to last for a few days.

These workers fitted wooden shutters to windows as Hurricane Hugo approached in 1989. ▷

Evacuation

The next morning, the hurricane is still on its way. A hurricane warning is broadcast. This means the hurricane is going to hit in the next 24 hours. People living right in the path of the hurricane are told to **evacuate** their homes.

There is no time to waste. Most people load their cars with supply kits, water, food, and pets. Then they head for the nearest **evacuation route.** Thousands of other people are leaving, too. It may take hours to get through the long traffic jams. When they reach safety, people try to find hotel rooms. Others camp out in their cars.

The most at risk areas in the United States have special places where people can take shelter. These are large, safe buildings, such as schools. The elderly are usually moved there first.

SUBJECT: Hurricane Watch
TIME: 6:00 P.M. Tuesday, May 6

The Hurricane Prediction Center has issued a hurricane watch for southern Florida. Hurricane Barbara (**category** 4) is predicted to hit land at 6:00 A.M. Thursday, May 8. **Sustained** winds of 150 miles (240 kilometers) per hour and a **storm surge** of 13 feet (4 meters) are likely. People in low-lying areas are advised to prepare to evacuate.

Follow the signs

In many hurricane hot spots, the authorities carefully figure out the best evacuation routes for people to take. This helps people to escape quickly. The routes are marked with special signs.

Evacuation routes often grind to a halt as thousands of people try to leave cities at the same time. ▽

EVACUATION ROUTE

evacuation route   path followed to get to a safe place

First signs

The hurricane is still hundreds of miles out at sea. Its **eye** will not arrive for many hours yet, but the hurricane is on its way. The wind is picking up. The waves crashing on the **shore** are getting larger. Gradually the sky clouds over.

Now it begins to rain. The rain lashes down for more than an hour. All the time the wind gets stronger. The waves get bigger and closer together. The **air pressure** is falling quickly. People can tell this by looking at their **barometers.** The eye of the storm is on its way!

Boats are often carried inland by storm surges. Cyclone Luis picked up this boat in 1995. ▽

△ Large waves created by Hurricane Felix crash into beach houses in Virginia in 1995.

barometer   instrument that measures air pressure
coast   land near a body of water

Storm surge

Now the sea level rises quickly. The **storm surge** has arrived. Overall, the sea rises 13 feet (4 meters) above its normal level. Soon the water is washing over the **coast**. It rushes through the empty streets into homes and shops. Everything is under water. Huge waves wash **inland**. They carry cars and parts of houses with them. Boats from the harbor are piled up in a parking lot. Buildings along the shore are destroyed by the waves. They collapse into the sea. Wooden houses float off their **foundations** and are severely damaged.

Snake trouble

Animals are also in danger from a storm surge. Snakes swim through the water, trying to find dry land. They are usually scared. They often bite if people get near them in the water.

△ Hurricane survivors can come face to face with scared snakes, like this Southern Pacific rattle snake.

foundation heavy base on which a building stands
shore land that is the border between a body of water and land

31

A Hurricane Arrives

Howling winds

The **eye** of the hurricane is just a few miles away. The **eye wall** is right overhead. This is the most violent part of the storm. The wind is screaming. Some gusts are traveling at more than 200 miles (320 kilometers) per hour. Rain is lashing down. Flashes of lightning streak across the dark sky.

The wind creates **havoc**. Trees tumble to the ground with their roots ripped out. The falling trees crush cars and houses. Telephone poles fall. Traffic lights and lampposts sway wildly. Cars roll and trucks flip over. The street is a dangerous place to be. Roof tiles, sheets of metal and plastic, signs, garden furniture, and other **debris** fly around. They are like deadly **missiles**.

Measuring the wind

It is often impossible to measure the strongest gusts of wind during a hurricane. Wind-measuring instruments, called anemometers, are normally destroyed by winds of more than 155 miles (250 kilometers) per hour.

Hurricane watchers took this photograph of a gas station in the middle of a hurricane. This is a dangerous hobby!

havoc great disorder and ruin

A couple examines the damage to their home in South Carolina after it was hit by Hurricane Hugo in 1989.

◁

Camille party

In 1969 a group of 25 people decided to stay in their apartments in Mississippi for a hurricane party. When Hurricane Camille hit, the wind and **storm surge** swept the apartment block away. Nobody survived.

The eye passes

Now the winds suddenly die down. The sky clears and the sun shines. The hurricane seems to have gone, but this should not fool you. The light winds and clear sky mean that the hurricane's eye has arrived. There will only be a short rest from the howling wind. After only half an hour the wind starts again. The eye has passed by. Now the wind blows from the southwest.

Small houses are ripped apart by the wind. Others lose their roofs. The winds tear through a town center. They pull windows from office blocks. Glass crashes into the streets below.

missile rocket used as a weapon

The hurricane ends

It is twelve hours since the hurricane's **eye** passed. The wind has died down. The sea is calm. There was more heavy rain, but now it has stopped. The sky is blue and the sun is shining. There is still seawater in the street. This poured **inland** during the **storm surge**. It is draining slowly back into the ocean.

Rebuilding Galveston

In 1900 Galveston, Texas, was destroyed by a hurricane. Galveston now has a 16.5-ft (5-m) wall along the **coast** to stop storm surges from coming inland.

△ The shattered remains of wooden houses in Galveston in 1900.

△ Mobile home parks are often completely wrecked by hurricane-force winds. This damage was caused by Hurricane Andrew in 1992.

bacteria   living things that can only be seen under a microscope
developing country   poor country that is trying to improve its living conditions

People who **evacuated** are returning home. They find **devastation** all around. The hurricane has completely destroyed some parts of the town. People who lived here have lost their homes. Their possessions have been ruined by seawater. The streets are full of mud and sand. Vehicles and boats lie in tangled piles.

Cleaning up

The hurricane caused all that damage in just a few hours, but it will take many months to clear up the mess. The emergency services begin to search for missing people. People without homes go to emergency shelters. The hurricane has damaged electricity supplies, telephone lines, and water pipes. These services are repaired as soon as possible. **Debris** is cleared from the streets. Builders begin repairing and rebuilding houses and other buildings.

Hurricane damage is often worse in **developing countries.** People have very little even before a hurricane hits. They may have nothing at all afterward. **Relief agencies** often help to rescue people. They provide food and clean water. They repair **communications** and homes.

Disease spreads

Disease is often a problem after a hurricane. **Sewage** from flooded drains and **bacteria** from rotting dead animals makes water dangerous to drink. Diseases can spread quickly.

Emergency water supplies waiting to be handed out after Hurricane Andrew.

relief agency group that helps people in need, usually in developing countries
sewage mixture of waste from toilets and drains

Going Inland

For people on the **coast,** the worst is over, but the hurricane does not stop there. It keeps on going **inland.** Remember that a hurricane gets its **energy** from the warm ocean water. When a hurricane moves over land, it cannot get any more energy. It begins to die down, but very slowly. It may last for many more days and do a lot more damage.

Wind and rain

Although the hurricane's winds lose strength, they still blow strongly enough to damage trees and buildings inland. However, **torrential** rain begins to fall, and it keeps falling for hours on end.

Hurricane facts

A hurricane can dump lots of water over land. Big hurricanes have been known to drop 49.2 inches (125 centimeters) of rain in a single day. Some places do not get that much rain in a whole year.

Flash floods

Streams and rivers fill up very quickly because so much rain falls. They overflow and flood the landscape. These are **flash floods.** They happen so quickly that people have no time to escape. Roads, bridges, farms, and buildings are washed away. The rain mixes with dirt to make mud. The mud slides down river valleys. It flows into buildings and turns solid.

Now the storm's winds have slowed down. It is no longer a hurricane, but a **tropical** storm. The storm moves north across the United States and then out to sea. It loses more energy and finally dies away.

Pinatubo mudslides

Typhoon Yuna crossed the Philippines in 1991. A volcano called Mount Pinatubo erupted at exactly the same time. The typhoon's rains mixed with ash from the eruption. This made a heavy **slurry**. It pushed in roofs and formed deadly **mudslides.** Hundreds of people were killed.

▽ Flash floods caused by hurricanes often catch people without warning. The owners of these cars have left them.

△ This is the sort of damage that a mudslide can do. This disaster happened in the Philippines in February 1992.

slurry   half-liquid mixture that is like mud or cement

Hurricane Mitch

Hurricane Mitch was a **category** 5 hurricane. It hit Central America in October 1998. Although the winds blew at more than 150 miles (240 kilometers) per hour, the rain from Hurricane Mitch did the most damage. Mitch moved slowly through the Caribbean. Then it slowed almost to a stop over Honduras. In one day it dropped 25 inches (63 centimeters) of rain on Honduras and its neighboring countries. These are all poor countries. Most people are farmers who live in simple homes.

October 31, 1998

Slide of Death

Hurricane Mitch's **torrential** rains have triggered a disaster in northwest Nicaragua. Inches of rain mixed with volcanic ash from the Casitas volcano formed a deadly **slurry.** This fell down the mountainside, burying thousands.

△ These survivors are wearing masks because of fumes from dead bodies. They escaped a mudslide in Nicaragua, caused by Hurricane Mitch.

△ This **satellite** image taken on October 26, 1998, shows Hurricane Mitch just off the **coast** of Honduras.

chaos total confusion
economy way a country makes money for its people

Floods and mudslides

The rains caused terrible floods. Rivers grew into raging **torrents**. They swept away houses, people, and animals. Some people were carried out to sea. Hillsides became soaked. Eventually they collapsed. This created powerful **mudslides** full of rock. They ripped through towns and killed about 10,000 people.

Mitch's devastation

Hurricane Mitch drifted away, the rain stopped, and the floods gradually drained away. They left behind a scene of muddy **chaos.** Tens of thousands of people had no houses, fresh water, food, or electricity. Roads and bridges were washed away. This made it almost impossible to get food, water, and medical supplies to victims. The United States helped Honduras **recover** by sending aid money.

Ruined economies

The **economies** of Honduras, Guatemala, and Costa Rica depend on **exports** of bananas, coffee, and sugarcane. Hurricane Mitch ruined these crops in 1998. The countries are still trying to get back to normal.

Guanaja in Honduras was **devastated** by Hurricane Mitch in 1998.

exports   goods sent out for sale in another country
torrent   rushing stream of liquid

Fighting Hurricanes

Dozens of people die in hurricanes every year. Hurricanes also cause millions of dollars of damage. We cannot stop hurricanes, but we can try to **forecast** where and when they will hit land. To forecast hurricanes, we need to know how they will act.

Hurricane forecasting

Pictures from weather **satellites** are very useful. They show the exact position of **seedlings**, **tropical** storms, and hurricanes. Hurricane **forecasters** can measure the size of the **eye** from them, too. Accurate measurements of wind speeds and **air pressures** are also needed. "Hurricane Hunter" aircraft fly into storms to collect this information. This **data** is then put into computer programs. These programs can **predict** where the hurricane will hit land. Then **meteorologists** can **broadcast** warnings.

Before satellites

The first weather satellites were launched into space in the 1960s. Before satellites, it was almost impossible for forecasters to keep track of hurricanes. So hurricanes often hit without warning.

This weather satellite sends back photographs of the **atmosphere** every half hour.

computer model   computer program used to predict things
Doppler radar   type of radar that can detect objects and measure speed

Hurricane research

Hurricanes are difficult for forecasters to predict. They often change speed direction or strength. Hurricanes often land in places where they are not expected. Researchers try to find out why hurricanes change direction. Here are some ways they do this:

- study measurements from previous hurricanes;
- find out how water temperatures change when hurricanes pass by;
- try to link the pattern of hurricanes with other world weather patterns, such as the **El Niño** ocean **current.**

Researchers use this information to make their **computer models** better. There is still a lot for researchers to find out and understand.

> Although there are usually some bumps on the way through, they are nothing that the airplane can't handle!
>
> Hurricane Hunter crew member

A giant thunderstorm such as this could be the first sign that a new hurricane is about to be born. ▽

Hurricane chasers measure wind speeds using a special instrument called a **Doppler radar.** △

El Niño   pattern of wind and ocean currents that brings extreme weather
forecast   give or predict information about something that might happen

Be prepared

Your chances of surviving a hurricane are quite high. In fact, nearly all people live to tell the tale. You are not likely to die if you are well prepared. You should plan what to do when a hurricane strikes. You must know where to listen for hurricane warnings. If you practice your escape plan regularly, you will remember what to do when the real thing happens. For example, you could ask your parents to drive along the **evacuation route.**

Safer and safer

More and more people are living in hurricane **hot spots.** About 15 percent of the world's **population** is at risk. But the number of people hurricanes kill and injure is decreasing. This is because of better **forecasting** and warnings.

△ Members of the U.S. Air Force track the progress of Hurricane Isabel in 2003.

Hurricane survival guide

- Check if you live in an evacuation area.
- Find out what would happen to your home if there were high winds, a **storm surge,** or flooding.
- Do not forget your pets.
- Prepare a survival kit.
- At the start of a hurricane season, check your supply kit and make sure your window and door shutters are ready.
- During the hurricane season, listen to weather forecasts regularly.
- If a hurricane is on the way, follow the advice given in warnings.
- Follow your family's disaster plan.
- **Evacuate** if you are asked to.

Controlling hurricanes

Many people ask if we can control hurricanes. Would it be possible to weaken a hurricane or make it change its path to miss people's homes? Weather experts have had some interesting ideas. One idea is to drop salt or ice into a hurricane. This could make the **eye** grow bigger. The winds become weaker when the **eye** is bigger. However, at the moment we don't understand hurricanes well enough to figure out how to control them. We could even make things worse.

Hurricane resistant

Are there buildings strong enough to resist hurricanes? The answer is yes. Skyscrapers, stadiums, and bridges must all be able to survive hurricane-force winds. But it is too expensive to make ordinary houses hurricane-proof.

Hong Kong's towering skyscrapers are designed to survive the winds that could hit during a **typhoon.** ▽

Find Out More

Books

Berger, Melvin, and Gilda Berger. *Hurricanes Have Eyes but Can't See: And Other Amazing Facts about Wild Weather.* New York: Scholastic, 2003.

Chambers, Catherine. *Disasters in Nature: Hurricanes.* Chicago: Heinemann Library, 2000.

Steele, Christy. *Nature on the Rampage: Hurricanes.* Chicago: Raintree, 2004.

World Wide Web

If you want to find out more about hurricanes, you can search the Internet using keywords such as these:

- hurricane + news + [date you are interested in]
- Bangladesh + **cyclones**
- wind + **El Niño** + hurricanes

You can also find your own keywords by using headings or words from this book. Use the search tips on the next page to help you find the most useful websites.

Organizations

The National Weather Service

An organization that keeps track of weather conditions around the country. The National weather service occasionally issues severe weather warnings when necessary. Contact them at the following address: National Weather Service, National Oceanic and Atmospheric Administration, US Dept. of Commerce, 1325 East West Highway, Silver Spring, MD 20910 www.nws.noaa.gov

Search tips

There are billions of pages on the Internet, so it can be difficult to find exactly what you want to find. For example, if you just type in "hurricane" on a search engine such as Google, you'll get a list of millions of web pages. These tips will help you find useful websites more quickly:

- Decide exactly what you want to find out about first.
- Use simple keywords instead of whole sentences.
- Use two to six keywords in a search, putting the most important words first.
- Be precise—use names of people, places, or things when you can.
- If your keywords are made up of two or more words that go together, put quote marks around them—for example, "Hurricane Mitch."
- Use the "+" sign to join keywords together—for example, "weather + disaster."

Where to search

Search engine

A search engine looks through millions of web pages and lists all the sites that match the words in the search box. They can give thousands of links, but the best matches are at the top of the list, on the first page. Try **google.com**.

Search directory

A search directory is more like a library of websites that have been sorted by a person instead of a computer. You can search by keyword or subject and browse through the different sites in the same way you would look through books on a library shelf. A good example is **yahooligans.com**.

Glossary

air pressure force of air pressing down on Earth

atmosphere layer of gases that surround Earth

bacteria living things that can only be seen under a microscope

barometer instrument that measures air pressure

broadcast send information over the radio or television

category group or class of things

chaos total confusion

clockwise direction that the hands of a clock move around

coast land near a body of water

communication way of giving and receiving information

compact packed closely together

computer model computer program used to predict things

condense turn from gas into liquid

counterclockwise moving in the opposite direction to the hands of a clock

cumulonimbus enormous thunder clouds up to 32,800 feet (10 kilometers) high

current steady flow of water or air in one direction

cyclone name given to a hurricane in the southern hemisphere

data information, usually in the form of facts or statistics

debris bits and pieces of wrecked houses, cars, and other objects

delta wide, fan-shaped piece of land, where a river empties into the sea

devastation damage and chaos after something violent happened

developing country poor country that is trying to improve its living conditions

Doppler radar type of radar that can detect objects and measure speed

economy way a country makes money for its people

El Niño pattern of wind and ocean currents that brings extreme weather

energy source that provides power

equator imaginary line around Earth, halfway between the poles

erosion wearing away by action of water or wind

evacuate leave home and go to a safe place

evacuation route path followed to get to a safe place

evaporate turn from liquid to gas

exports goods sent out for sale in another country

eye area in the center of a hurricane where the winds are calm

eye wall wall of tall clouds around the eye of a hurricane

flash flood quickly developing flood

forecast   give or predict information about something that might happen

forecaster   person who figures out what the weather will be like in the future

foundation   heavy base on which a building stands

havoc   great disorder and ruin

hemisphere   one half of Earth

hot spot   place where something happens often

inland   away from the coast

intensity   strength

international   used in or to do with many countries

landslide   fast movement of materials, such as earth and rock, down a slope

latitude   distance north or south of the equator, measured in degrees

meteorologist   scientist who studies and reports on the weather

missile   rocket used as a weapon

mudslide   mixture of water and earth that slides down a hillside or river

paddy   water-filled field used for growing rice

population   total number of people living in a place

predict   say what will happen in the future

recover   get better

relief agency   group that helps people in need, usually in developing countries

rotate   turn around or twist

satellite   object that observes Earth from space

season   time of the year with typical weather

seedling   group of thunderstorms that may turn into a hurricane

severe   very bad or serious

sewage   mixture of waste from toilets and drains

shore   land that is the border between a body of water and land

slurry   half-liquid mixture that is like mud or cement

storm surge   sudden rise in sea level that happens as a hurricane approaches land

suburb   area of houses on the edge of a city

surge   sudden rush

sustain   keep at a certain strength or level all the time

tornado   spinning column of air that makes contact with the ground

torrent   rushing stream of liquid

torrential   like a torrent, which is a rushing stream of liquid

tropical   in the area of the world, near the equator, where the weather is warm

typhoon   name given to a hurricane in the western North Pacific

updraft   rising air

water vapor   water in the form of a gas

Index